Mushrooms

Mushrooms

SECOND EDITION

Todd Telander

FALCON GUIDES

ESSEX, CONNECTICUT

To my wife, Kirsten, my children, Miles and Oliver, and my parents, who all have supported and encouraged me through the years

FALCONGUIDES®

An imprint of Globe Pequot, the trade division of
The Rowman & Littlefield Publishing Group, Inc.
4501 Forbes Blvd., Ste. 200
Lanham, MD 20706
www.rowman.com

Falcon and FalconGuides are registered trademarks and
Make Adventure Your Story is a trademark of
The Rowman & Littlefield Publishing Group, Inc.

Distributed by NATIONAL BOOK NETWORK

British Library Cataloguing in Publication Information available

Library of Congress Cataloging-in-Publication Data

Names: Telander, Todd, author.
Title: Mushrooms / Todd Telander.
Other titles: Falcon field guide.
Description: Second edition | Essex, Connecticut : Falcon Guides, [2023] | Series: A Falcon field guide. | Includes index.
Identifiers: LCCN 2022043728 (print) | LCCN 2022043729 (ebook) | ISBN 9781493065585 (paperback) | ISBN 9781493065592 (epub)
Subjects: LCSH: Mushrooms—North America—Identification. | Field guides.
Classification: LCC QK604.5 .T45 2023 (print) | LCC QK604.5 (ebook) | DDC 579.6097—dc23/eng/20220920
LC record available at https://lccn.loc.gov/2022043728
LC ebook record available at https://lccn.loc.gov/2022043729

♾️™ The paper used in this publication meets the minimum requirements of American National Standard for Information Sciences—Permanence of Paper for Printed Library Materials, ANSI/NISO Z39.48-1992.

The author and The Rowman & Littlefield Publishing Group, Inc. assume no liability for accidents happening to, or injuries sustained by, readers who engage in the activities described in this book.

Contents

Introduction

Mushrooms are a mysterious and beautiful group of organisms. They seem to magically appear from nowhere, are found in almost every environment, and can take almost every form imaginable. Add to that the fact that some are highly prized as food, whereas some can kill you, and you have the makings for a fascinating and fulfilling area of study and exploration. This guide is an overview of some of the most common and interesting mushrooms that can be found within the United States, including many that are considered edible and some that are poisonous. It is not meant to be a definitive guide to identification, so be sure to consult an expert before attempting to ingest any mushroom.

Note: Collectors should inquire regarding local regulations on public lands prior to doing any collecting, especially in national parks where collecting and consuming wild plants is generally prohibited.

Names

Each entry includes the common name as well as the scientific name. Because common names tend to vary regionally, or because there may be more than one common name for each species, the universally accepted scientific name of genus and species (such as *Lactarius deliciosus* for the Delicious Milk Cap) is more reliable to be certain of identification. Note that some species may have two or even three accepted scientific names. It's worth mentioning that one can often learn interesting facts about a fungus from the English translation of its Latin name.

Size

There is great variability in the height and width of mushrooms, even within the same species. For the sake of simplicity, each entry includes the average largest height and width that you are likely to see. Note that many will be smaller, especially if they are early in development, and that some may exceed these measurements.

Spore Print

With many mushroom species, if you separate the cap and place it on a clean, white surface, a print of a certain color will form after a few hours. This print is made from the spores dropping out from the gills or pores and can be a good indicator of species or genus.

Descriptions

Describing a mushroom can be a complicated affair because of the great degree of variability in shape, texture, and color. Also, most mushrooms go through several stages during their development, each of which may look completely different. With this in mind, I have included descriptions of the most noticeable forms of each species, especially in relation to changes in cap shape, color, and emergence of structures such as scales, collars, and volvas.

Habitat, Range, and Season

It is helpful to note the habitat, range, and season of a mushroom to aid in identification. Some are found almost everywhere, but others are quite restricted by their environment and appear only in specific locales and seasons.

Edibility

Most of the species listed in this guide are edible, but there is much variation as to their flavor or desirability. Some that have good flavor may be palatable only if they are cooked and certain parts are removed, whereas others may be too small to amount to anything. Of course, personal taste is the ultimate judge, so where some people may find a species choice, others may find it distasteful or bland. Surprisingly, many mushrooms are still not known well enough to safely determine edibility. If a species is poisonous or causes illness, I have indicated that. As mentioned earlier, **please do not attempt to eat any mushroom unless you are absolutely sure of its identity and you have the assistance of an expert. If you do decide to consume a mushroom, always begin with small bits and cook them well.**

Illustrations

The illustrations generally depict each species in its mature form and color. If immature forms are quite different, I have also included those. Remember that because many species show great diversity, an illustration alone should never suffice for identification.

Mushroom Morphology

On the next page is a diagram of a typical mushroom of the order Agaricales, or the common "toadstool" form. It consists of a cap, stalk, base, and sometimes a collar and basal volva. This is the fruiting body of the fungus, which is only the visible part of a large network of rootlike filaments that grows underground throughout the year. Under the cap, a series of gills or tubes produces spores that are released and propagate the species. Other orders of mushrooms, such as bracket fungi, club fungi, puffballs, and morels, do not have this typical shape and form and are thus described in the species accounts. Mushrooms, unlike plants, do not utilize photosynthesis to produce nutrients; they rely on decaying matter in the soil or wood on which they live.

Gill Attachment

For many mushrooms, the fashion by which the gills attach to the stalk is a good field mark to identification. If the gills meet the stalk directly, they are considered attached. If they do not meet the stalk, they are considered free. They may also descend downward to meet the stalk far below the cap, and this condition is sometimes called "decurrent."

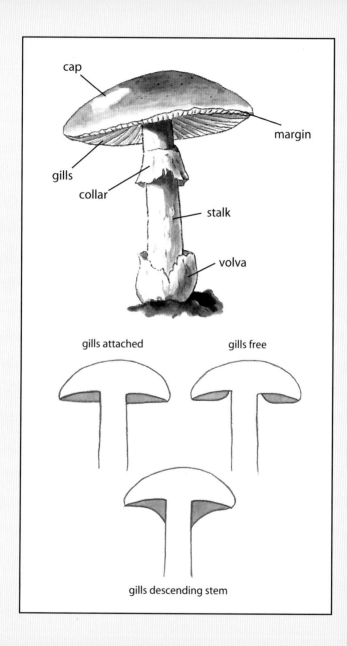

Chocolate Milky, *Lactarius lignyotus*
Family: Russulaceae (Milk Caps)
Height to 5"
Spore print: Yellow or ochre

Cap is up to 4" wide, convex with a prominent central knob, becoming flattened and the cap's margin becoming wavy with age. Surface is dry and velvety, sometimes wrinkled in the center and chocolate brown. Stalk is dark brown, white at the base, and sometimes lightly striated. Gills are attached or descending on the stalk, white at first and becoming darker with age. Flesh emits a white, milky latex when cut. The Chocolate Milky is found in coniferous woodlands near rotting wood in eastern North America during the late summer and fall. It is edible but not recommended.

Bleeding Milk Cap, *Lactarius rubrilacteus*
Family: Russulaceae (Milk Caps)
Height to 2½"
Spore print: Pale yellow or cream-colored

Cap is up to 5" wide, convex and depressed in the center, becoming flattened and more depressed with age. Colored in concentric zones of tan, brown, or bright orange, sometimes with darker greenish spots, and exuding a reddish latex when cut. Margin is wavy. The stalk is colored as the cap and about equal diameter throughout its length. Gills are attached, often descending down the stalk, and colored pale reddish-brown. The Bleeding Milk Cap is found in coniferous woodlands in western North America during the summer and fall. It is edible but not recommended. Also known as the Red-juice Milky Cap.

Delicious Milk Cap, *Lactarius deliciosus*
Family: Russulaceae (Milk Caps)
Height to 2¾"
Spore print: Cream-colored

Cap is up to 5" wide, convex to flat, depressed in the middle with an incurved margin, becoming funnel-shaped with age. Color is orange or beige with concentric darker orange rings. Flesh will stain red then greenish where bruised. Stalk is thick and colored pale orange. Gills are attached and descend partly down the stalk. The flesh exudes an orange, milky latex when cut. The Delicious Milk Cap is found in pine forests throughout North America during the fall. It is edible but not necessarily considered delicious. Also known as the Orange Milky, Saffron Milk Cap, and Red Pine Mushroom.

Orange-brown Milky, *Lactifluus volemus*
Family: Russulaceae (Milk Caps)
Height to 4"
Spore print: White

Cap is up to 5" wide, convex, depressed in the center with a flat or incurved margin. Color is a uniform reddish-orange. Stalk is straight, smooth, and pale orange-brown. Gills are attached and cream-colored. When cut, the flesh exudes latex that is white initially and then turns brown. It has a somewhat fishy odor. The Orange-brown Milky is found in deciduous woodlands in eastern North America during the summer and fall. Edible and quite good. Also known as the Voluminous-latex Milky.

Cottony-margined Milky Cap, *Lactarius deceptivus*
Family: Russulaceae (Milk Caps)
Height to 3½"
Spore print: White to buff

The large cap is up to 10" wide, white, and convex with a depression in the middle or vase-shaped. Margin is inrolled and textured like cotton. Stalk is thick, straight, white, stiff, and brittle. Gills are attached and colored white or pale brown. When cut, the flesh exudes a white, milky latex. The Cottony-margined Milky Cap is found near moss in mixed woodlands in central and eastern North America during the summer and early fall. It is edible if cooked but quite acrid in taste. Also known as the Deceptive Milky.

Indigo Milk Cap, *Lactarius indigo*
Family: Russulaceae (Milk Caps)
Height to 3"
Spore print: Cream-colored

Cap is up to 6" wide, convex with a depressed center and inrolled margin. Surface is smooth and has a unique coloring of bright bluish to gray with concentric banding. Stalk is straight along its length or slightly narrowing at the base. Gills are attached, descending down the stalk, and blue or gray. Flesh is brittle and exudes a dark, indigo-blue latex when cut. The Indigo Milk Cap is found on the ground near oak or pine woods in southeastern North America during the summer and fall. It is edible.

Emetic Russula, *Russula emitica* ☠
Family: Russulaceae (Milk Caps)
Height to 4"
Spore print: White to pale yellow

Cap is slimy and bright red-orange, growing to 4" wide. It begins convex and becomes flat to concave with a sunken center and upcurved outer margin. Gills are white to creamy, attached, and closely spaced. Stalk is thick, white, and brittle and lacks a collar ring. The Emetic Russula prefers to grow in boggy areas near pine woodlands during the late summer or fall throughout North America. Poisonous and emetic (causes vomiting).

Short-stemmed Russula, *Russula brevipes*
Family: Russulaceae (Milk Caps)
Height to 6"
Spore print: White or cream-colored

Cap is up to 8" wide, convex with a depressed center, and colored white to off-white or brownish. The stalk is very short, thick, and stubby; white or cream-colored. Gills are attached, descending down the stalk, and white or stained brownish. The Short-stemmed Russula is found in mixed woodlands throughout North America during the summer and fall. It is edible but not particularly flavorful.

Shellfish-scented Russula, *Russula xerampelina*
Family: Russulaceae (Milk Caps)
Height to 4½"
Spore print: Yellow to ochre

Cap is up to 6" wide, convex to flattened, and slightly depressed in the center, colored purple to reddish-brown or even greenish. Stalk is white or washed with pink or purple and quite brittle. Gills are attached, pale, or bruised with brown. Odor is sweet and fishy, especially in older specimens. The Shellfish-scented Russula is found on the ground in mixed woodlands throughout North America during the summer and fall. It is edible and very tasty. Also known as the Shrimp Russula and Woodland Russula.

Golden Waxy Cap, *Hygrophorus flavescens* or *Hygrocybe flavescens*
Family: Hygrophoraceae (Waxy Caps)
Height to 3½"
Spore print: White

Cap is up to 3" wide, convex, and becoming flattened with age. Surface is smooth and sticky and colored bright yellow to yellow-orange. Stalk is smooth, equal along its length, and colored as the cap, becoming paler toward the base. Gills are free or partly attached, descending down the stalk, pale yellow and waxy. The Golden Waxy Cap is found in moist areas with humus in mixed woodlands during the summer and fall in eastern North America or during the winter in California. It is edible but insubstantial.

White Waxy Cap, *Hygrophorus eburneus*
Family: Hygrophoraceae (Waxy Caps)
Height to 6"
Spore print: White

Cap is up to 4" wide, convex, and becoming flattened with a depressed center. Surface is white or ivory and sticky or slimy when wet. Stalk is fairly thin, white, and slimy like the cap. Gills are attached, descending slightly down the stalk, and white and waxy. Collar is usually not present. The White Waxy Cap is found in fields or mixed woodlands in northern North America and in California during the fall and winter. It is edible, although the texture may be unappetizing. Also known as the Ivory Waxy Cap.

Witch's Hat, *Hygrocybe conica* ☠
Family: Hygrophoraceae (Waxy Caps)
Height to 6"
Spore print: White

Cap is up to 3½" across, sharply conical (like a witch's hat), becoming flatter with age but maintaining a conical center. Surface is waxy or tacky and a reddish-orange that is lighter toward the margin. Stalk is thin and straight, paler than the cap, and lined with vertical striations. Gills are free to partly attached and pale yellow or darker. All flesh becomes black with age. The Witch's Hat is found in coniferous woodlands throughout North America during most of the year. Edibility is questionable; the mushroom is considered poisonous by some.

Russula-like Waxy Cap, *Hygrophorus russula*
Family: Hygrophoraceae (Waxy Caps)
Height to 3"
Spore print: White

Cap is up to 5" wide, convex, and becoming flattened with age. Surface is sticky or waxy when moist, pale pinkish or purplish, and sometimes showing thin, purple striations. Margin is inrolled and paler. Stalk is smooth and colored as the cap. Gills are attached, white to pale purple, and not descending down the stalk. The Russula-like Waxy Cap is found on the ground in deciduous woodlands, particularly those with oak, throughout North America during the fall, and is sometimes seen during the winter in California. It is edible. Also known as the False Russula.

Parrot Waxy Cap, *Gliophorus psittacinus*
Family: Hygrophoraceae (Waxy Caps)
Height to 3½"
Spore print: White

Cap is up to 2" wide, dome-shaped to convex or flattened. The color resembles that of a parrot: bright green turning yellow-brown to darker brown with age. Margin is thin and pale with striations. Stalk is yellow-green, becoming yellow or brown. Gills are attached, waxy, and a green that fades in color like the cap. The Parrot Waxy Cap is found on the ground in mixed woodlands and pastures throughout North America during the summer and fall or during the winter in California. The mushroom is edible but not great. Also known as the Parrot Mushroom.

Fading Scarlet Waxy Cap, *Hygrocybe miniata*
Family: Hygrophoraceae (Waxy Caps)
Height to 3"
Spore print: White

This small mushroom has a cap up to 1½" wide, convex, becoming flattened with age (not cone-shaped like the Witch's Hat). Surface is a bright scarlet fading to yellow or orange, shiny but not sticky or waxy. Stalk is thin and equal along its length and colored like the cap. Gills are attached, waxy, yellow-orange, and broad. The Fading Scarlet Waxy Cap is found near mossy areas in mixed woodlands throughout North America during the summer and fall or during the winter in California. It is edible but lacks flavor and substance. Also known as the Miniature Waxy Cap or Vermillion Waxcap.

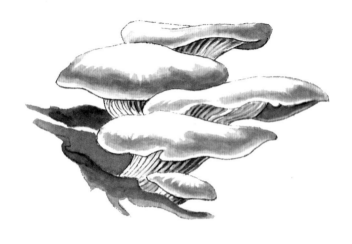

Oyster Mushroom, *Pleurotus ostreatus*
Family: Pleurotaceae
Width to 3½"
Spore print: White or very pale purple

Cap is wavy, convex to flattened, shaped somewhat like an oyster shell, white to brownish or gray, and fleshy. The stalk is minimal or absent and usually off-center. Gills are white to yellowish, descending all the way down to a tough base. The Oyster Mushroom grows in clusters, shelflike, from the bark of trees or fallen logs. The mushroom is found in mixed woodlands throughout North America during most seasons. It is edible and very good. Also known as the Hiratake.

Jack-o-lantern, *Omphalotus olearius* ☠
Family: Marasmiaceae
Height to 8"
Spore print: Cream-colored

Cap is up to 8" wide, convex, and becoming flattened to funnel-shaped, smooth, and bright yellow-orange. Stalk is thin, often tapering toward the base, and sometimes off-center. Gills are attached, thin-edged, descending down the stalk, colored as the cap, and may be seen glowing green in the dark. The Jack-o-lantern grows on stumps and roots in mixed woodlands, often forming clusters. It is found during the summer and fall in eastern North America or during the winter in California. The mushroom is poisonous and causes stomach upset; caution must be taken not to confuse it with the similar-looking chanterelle.

Funnel Clitocybe, *Clitocybe gibba* or *Infundibulicybe gibba* ☠
Family: Tricholomataceae
Height to 3"
Spore print: White

Cap is up to 3" wide, flat with a depressed center to deeply funnel-shaped. Surface is smooth and pale reddish-brown with a wavy margin. Stalk is thin, smooth, and whitish. Gills are attached, descending far down the stalk, and white or ivory. The Funnel Clitocybe is found on the ground in coniferous or deciduous woodlands throughout North America during the summer and fall or during the winter in California. Not edible. Also known as the Funnel Cap.

Blewit, *Clitocybe nuda*
Family: Tricholomataceae
Height to 3½"
Spore print: Pale pink to tan-pink

Cap is up to 6" wide, convex, and then flattened or depressed in the center. Surface is smooth, pale purple or bluish-purple, becoming light brown. Margin is inrolled when young, and upturned and undulating in older specimens. The stalk is thick, becoming bulbous at the base, and pale pinkish-purple. Gills are pale purple or light brown and partly attached, slightly descending down the stalk. Flesh has a strong, sweet odor. The Blewit is found on the ground in open woodlands or in gardens and compost piles throughout North America during the fall or during the winter in California. It is edible and very good.

Club-footed Clitocybe, *Ampulloclitocybe clavipes*
Family: Hygrophoraceae
Height to 3"
Spore print: White

Cap is up to 4" wide, convex, and then flattened or depressed in the center. Surface is smooth and colored a bland gray-brown, slightly lighter near the margin. Stalk is quite thick and markedly bulbous at the base, off-white or grayish. Gills are white, attached, and descending down the stalk. The Club-footed Clitocybe grows on the ground, singly or in groups, in mixed coniferous or deciduous woodlands throughout North America during the summer and fall or during the winter in California. It is edible but may cause illness if consumed with alcohol. Also known as the Clubfoot.

Waxy Laccaria, *Laccaria laccata*
Family: Hydnangiaceae
Height to 4"
Spore print: White

Cap is up to 2" wide, convex to flattened, and wavy with a con-cave depression in the center. Surface is reddish-orange or pink-ish and may be minutely scaled and velvety. Margin is thin and frilled. Stalk is thin, spindly, tough, equal in width along its length, and colored as the cap. Gills are thick and well-spaced, descend-ing slightly down the stalk, and pink or pale orange-brown. The Waxy Laccaria is found in areas of poor or sandy soil under pines throughout North America during the summer and fall. It is edi-ble. Also known as the Common Laccaria and Lackluster Laccaria.

Canary Trich, *Tricholoma flovovirens* or *Tricholoma equestre*
Family: Tricholomataceae
Height to 4"
Spore print: White

Cap is up to 5" wide and convex, becoming flattened. Surface is sticky or slimy, with subtle scales, and yellow with a reddish-brown center. Stalk is thick, sometimes enlarging at the base, and colored pale, dull yellow. Gills are pale yellow and partly attached with a notch at the stalk. The Canary Trich grows in sandy or grassy areas, often under pine trees, throughout North America during the fall or during the winter in California. The mushroom is edible and very good. Also known as the Man-on-Horseback and Sandy Trich.

Honey Mushroom, *Armillaria mellea*
Family: Physalacriaceae
Height to 6"
Spore print: White

Cap is up to 5" wide, highly variable in shape but generally convex or flat, centrally depressed with an undulating margin. Surface is usually honey-colored, darker in the center, and covered with minute, fuzzy scales. Stalk is pale above and darker brown below, with a somewhat bulbous base, and has a white, membranous collar with a cottony margin. Gills are attached and descending down the stalk, white to brownish. The Honey Mushroom grows on decaying stumps and logs or on living trees, often forming large clusters. It is found throughout North America during the late summer and fall or during the winter in California. The mushroom is edible if cooked and the stalk is removed, but care must be taken to not confuse it with similar poisonous species. Also known as the Honey Fungus.

Fairy Ring Mushroom, *Marasmius oreades*
Family: Marasmiaceae
Height to 3"
Spore print: White or pale buff

Cap is up to 2" wide, convex or bell-shaped, becoming flattened, with a wavy, slightly striated margin, and colored variable shades of white to brown. Stalk is thin, spindly, and tough with tiny fuzzy hairs. Gills are free or partly attached, pale tan, thin, and well-spaced. The Fairy Ring Mushroom is common on urban lawns, sometimes forming groups in a wide circle, or "fairy ring." It grows throughout North America during the late spring to fall or during the winter in California. The mushroom is edible with the stalk removed, but care should be taken not to confuse it with poisonous look-alikes. Also known as the Scotch Bonnet.

Velvet Foot, *Flammulina velutipes*
Family: Physalacriaceae
Height to 4"
Spore print: White

Cap is up to 2" wide, convex to flattened with a central knob. Surface is smooth, tacky, or slimy, and colored golden brown or reddish, being darker in the center. Stalk is equal in width along its length, pale brown, with tiny hairs giving a velvetlike dark fuzz toward the base. Gills are attached or partly attached, whitish or creamy. The Velvet Foot often grows in clusters around rotting logs and stumps in deciduous woodlands throughout North America. It is found during seasons when other mushrooms are dormant, late summer through early spring. It is edible. Also known as the Velvet Stem and Enokitake.

Fuzzy Foot, *Xeromphalina campanella* ☠
Family: Marasmiaceae
Height to 2"
Spore print: Pale yellow-brown

This very small, delicate mushroom has a cap up to 1" wide that is convex with a depressed center and radial striping, colored golden brown to reddish with a paler margin. Stalk is thin, often with a bulbous base, and covered with thin dark hairs below. Gills descend the stalk and are widely spaced and pale brownish-yellow. The Fuzzy Foot is found on decaying wood in coniferous woodlands throughout North America during the summer and fall. Not edible. Also known as the Golden Trumpet.

Blusher, *Amanita rubescens*
Family: Amanitaceae (Amanitas)
Height to 7"
Spore print: White

Cap is cream-colored to red-brown with pale or dark pinkish scale patches, up to 6" in diameter. Shape is ovoid, becoming convex to flat, with a slight rising knob in the center. Gills are free or slightly attached. Stalk is smooth, white above fading to reddish-brown toward the basal bulb, with a white to pinkish membranous collar ring. When bruised, the flesh is pink or red. The Blusher is found in open woodlands with good sun during the fall or winter in eastern North America and California. It is edible with caution for poisonous look-alikes.

Citron Amanita, *Amanita citrina*
Family: Amanitaceae (Amanitas)
Height to 5"
Spore print: White

Cap is pale greenish to yellow, convex, up to 4" wide with pale buff patches of veil remnants. Stalk is whitish with a draping collar ring and a large, cupped basal bulb. Gills are crowded, free, or slightly attached. The Citron Amanita is found in oak or pine woodlands throughout eastern North America during the fall. This is a dangerous mushroom to eat because of its close resemblance to the deadly death cap mushroom, *Amanita phalloides*.

Panther, *Amanita pantherina* ☠

Family: Amanitaceae (Amanitas)
Height to 6"
Spore print: White

Cap is white to light brown or yellowish with pale wart patches, looking like the hide of a panther. It is convex, becoming flat to depressed in the center with age. Gills are white and free or slightly attached. Stalk is tapered, white, with a membranous, pendant collar. One or more concentric ridges form just above the basal bulb. The Panther is found in deciduous or coniferous forests, most commonly in the Rocky Mountains or Pacific Northwest during the summer or fall. Poisonous.

Fly Agaric, *Amanita muscaria* ☠

Family: Amanitaceae (Amanitas)
Height to 7"
Spore print: White

Cap is hemispherical to flat to slightly concave and up to 10" in diameter with a striated margin. Flesh is smooth and red-orange with white wart patches sometimes arranged concentrically around the cap. Gills are free and white. Stalk is white and thick with a membranous, pendant collar ring. Just above the basal bulb are bands of veil remnants or scales. The Fly Agaric grows in mountainous, mixed woodlands of the Northwest and the Rocky Mountains during the late summer. California individuals grow during the winter. Very poisonous. The common name derives from the practice of combining the mushroom with milk to cause stupor in flies.

Caesar's Mushroom, *Amanita caesarea*
Family: Amanitaceae (Amanitas)
Height to 7"
Spore print: White
Cap is up to 8" wide, convex, and becoming flattened, with a finely striated margin. Surface is bright red-orange, darkest in the center, fading overall with age. Stalk is smooth or with small scales and colored as the cap, with a membranous collar that hangs skirtlike under the cap. At the base is a white, saclike volva. Gills are free or partly attached, cream or yellowish. The Caesar's Mushroom grows singly or in fairy rings in pine or oak woodlands in eastern and southwestern North America during the summer and fall. It is edible with caution to avoid poisonous look-alikes. Also known as the American Caesar's Mushroom.

Death Cap, *Amanita phalloides* ☠
Family: Amanitaceae (Amanitas)
Height to 6"
Spore print: White

This deadly mushroom has a cap up to 6" wide, convex to flattened, smooth, and colored variable shades of green to pale brown, darker toward the center. Stalk is pale green, sometimes scaly, and enlarged at the base where it arises out of a white, cup-shaped volva. There is a membranous, skirtlike collar below the cap. Gills are free or slightly attached, white to pale green. The Death Cap grows on the ground in a variety of habitats, including mixed woodlands (especially oak) and lawns, throughout North America during the late fall and early winter. It is poisonous and deadly.

Grisette, *Amanita vaginata*
Family: Amanitaceae (Amanitas)
Height to 6"
Spore print: White

Cap is up to 4" wide, convex or bell-shaped to flattened or upturned with a raised, central knob. Surface is various shades of pale brown or gray, smooth, and often with one or more patches of white veil tissue. The margin is clearly grooved. Stalk is thin, pale grayish-brown, sometimes with small scales, and based in a saclike volva. A collar is usually lacking. Gills are free or partly attached and whitish. The Grisette is found in a variety of habitats, including grassy areas and woodlands throughout North America during the spring and fall or during the winter in California. It is edible with caution for poisonous look-alikes. Also known as the Sheathed Amanita.

Destroying Angel, *Amanita virosa* ☠
Family: Amanitaceae (Amanitas)
Height to 8"
Spore print: White

Cap is up to 5" wide, convex to flattened, smooth, bright white (which may darken in the center with age), and has a smooth margin. Stalk is white with a shaggy, cottony surface and a delicate, papery, skirtlike collar that may be absent in older specimens. The base is bulbous and joins into a saclike volva. Gills are white and free or partly attached. The Destroying Angel grows on the ground in grassy areas and mixed woodlands throughout North America during the summer and fall. It is poisonous and deadly. Also known as the Death Angel, it is one of many related species that carries this name.

Parasol Mushroom, *Macrolepiota procera*
Family: Agaricaceae
Height to 16"
Spore print: White

This very large mushroom has a cap up to 8" wide, whitish to pale brown, ovoid, becoming flattened with age and having a distinct darker button in the middle. Concentric darker brownish scales, more concentrated in the center, dot the surface, and the margin is fringed. Gills are free and white or light brown. Stalk is tall and slender, light brown, and has variable scales and stripes. The collar is bandlike and moves freely up and down the stem if loosened. The Parasol is found in meadows and woodlands in eastern North America during the late summer. It is edible and tasty.

Smooth Lepiota, *Leucoagricus leucothites*
Family: Agaricaceae
Height to 6"
Spore print: White to pale pink

Cap is up to 6", hemispherical, becoming convex with maturity, white or off-white to grayish, and usually quite smooth, lacking scales or warts. Gills are white (browning with age), free, and dense. Stalk is white, smooth, and tapered slightly near the top. Collar is double-edged and moves freely on the stalk when loosened. The Smooth Lepiota is commonly found in gardens, lawns, and fields throughout North America during the fall and winter. It is edible with caution.

Shaggy Parasol, *Chlorophyllum rhacodes*
Family: Agaricaceae
Height to 8"
Spore print: White

Cap is large, up to 8" wide, and convex to nearly flat with age. It begins with concentric pinkish to rusty-colored scale bands that crack apart and disperse during growth, so the mature cap shows more white flesh overall. Margin is ragged and scaly. Gills are white and free. Stalk is fairly thick, white to brown, with a bulbous base and a double-edged, thin collar. The Shaggy Parasol grows singly or in fairy rings throughout North America in the fall. Edible with caution, as it may cause stomach upset.

False Chanterelle, *Hygrophoropsis aurantiaca*
Family: Hygrophoropidaceae
Height to 4"
Spore print: White

Cap is up to 3" wide, convex, flat, becoming funnel-shaped with age, with a somewhat inrolled margin. Surface is dry and pale to dark yellow-brown. Stalk is often bent, fleshy, colored as the cap, and becoming quite dark in contrast to the gills. Gills are attached, orange, descending down the stalk, and forked. The False Chanterelle grows in coniferous woodlands throughout North America during the fall. Edibility is questionable.

Pig's Ears, *Gomphus clavatus*
Family: Gomphaceae
Height to 8"
Spore print: Tan to ochre

The Pig's Ears begins cylindrical with a flattened top, becoming deeply vase- or funnel-shaped with an extremely undulating margin and interior, to 4" wide. Color is purplish to tan or brown. The fertile surface is pale purplish or yellow-brown and composed of interweaving veins from cap to base. The mushroom grows on the ground, often forming clumps, in coniferous woodlands during the fall in northern regions, the Pacific Northwest, and California. It is edible and very good. Also known as the Pig's Ears Gomphus or Violet Chanterelle.

Green-spored Parasol, *Chlorophyllum molybdites* ☠

Family: Agaricaceae
Height to 10"
Spore print: Dull olive-green

This large mushroom has a cap up to 12" wide, initially round and then conical to convex and flattened with age. Surface is covered with light brown scales, concentrated toward the center. Stalk is smooth and white to gray, becoming slightly bulbous at the base, and encircled by a white, membranous, moveable collar. Gills are free, whitish, becoming darker at maturity. The Green-spored Parasol grows on the ground, sometimes forming fairy rings, in pastures, meadows, and other grassy areas throughout North America during the fall. Not edible: poisonous! Also known as the Green-gilled Lepiota and False Parasol.

Meadow Mushroom, *Agaricus campestris*
Family: Agaricaceae
Height to 2½"
Spore print: Dark brown

Cap is up to 6" wide, convex, becoming flattened, smooth, white to pale gray-brown, and sometimes with soft, fibrous scales. Stalk is stout, tapering toward the base, white with scaling below, and encircled by a thin, membranous collar that leaves a transient ring. Gills are free, crowded, and pinkish, turning dark brown. The Meadow Mushroom is found in fields, lawns, and pastures throughout North America during the summer and fall or during the winter in California. It is edible and excellent, raw or cooked. Also known as the Pink Bottom and Field Mushroom.

Yellow-staining Agaricus, *Agaricus xanthodermus* ☠

Family: Agaricaceae
Height to 5"
Spore print: Dark brown

Cap is up to 7" wide, spherical, becoming convex and then flattened with age. Surface is smooth to scaly, white to dull gray-brown, being slightly darker in the center. Stalk is colored as the cap, somewhat bulbous at the base, with a substantial, pendant collar. Gills are free, starting out white and then turning dull pink and finally dark brown. Flesh turns bright yellow when bruised or cut. The Yellow-staining Agaricus grows in gardens, fields, and urban areas in the Pacific Northwest during the fall and in California during the winter. It is inedible and poisonous. Also known as the Yellow-foot Agaricus.

Horse Mushroom, *Agaricus arvensis*
Family: Agaricaceae
Height to 5"
Spore print: Dark brown

Cap is up to 3" wide, spherical, then becoming convex to flattened, smooth, and creamy white to pale yellow. It may have small scales, especially in the center, and the margin often retains pieces of papery veil remnants. Stalk is thick, enlarged toward the base, whitish, and with scales below the skirtlike collar. Gills are free, pale grayish, becoming dark brown. The flesh turns yellow when bruised and has an aniselike odor. The Horse Mushroom sometimes forms fairy rings in lawns and pastures throughout North America during the summer and fall or during the winter in California. It is edible and very good.

Glistening Inky Cap, *Coprinellus micaceus*
Family: Psathyrellaceae (Ink Caps and others)
Height to 3½"
Spore print: Black

Cap is up to 2" wide when open, round or oval to bell-shaped or convex, and striated nearly to the center. Surface is ochre or brownish, shiny when wet, and covered with small, glistening scales that are lost upon maturity. Stalk is thin, smooth, and white. Gills are grayish, becoming black and liquefying (as with most of the "inky caps"). The Glistening Inky Cap often grows in clumps on lawns and decaying wood throughout North America during the spring and fall. It is edible but insubstantial. Also known as the Mica Cap and Shiny Cap.

Shaggy Mane, *Coprinus comatus*
Family: Agaricaceae
Height to 10"
Spore print: Black

This large, white to pale reddish-brown mushroom begins
sausage-shaped and then resembles a pine cone, with ragged,
peeling scales. Eventually it becomes bell-shaped and liquefies
into a black goo. Stalk is smooth, tall, slightly thicker near the
base, and encircled by a thin, moveable collar that also liquefies
black with age. Gills are free, white at first and then becoming
black liquid. The Shaggy Mane is found in a variety of grassy or
dirt areas throughout North America during the spring and fall or
during the winter in the Southeast. It is edible and very good but
best when young.

Inky Cap, *Coprinopsis atramentarius*
Family: Psathyrellaceae (Ink Caps and others)
Height to 6"
Spore print: Black

Cap is up to 3" wide, grayish or pale brown, darkest near the margin, and oval to bell-shaped or convex. Surface is finely grooved and the margin striated. Stalk is whitish, smooth, and hollow, with an insubstantial, papery collar zone. Gills are free, dense, and white, becoming gray-pink and then black. As in other inky caps, the flesh liquefies with maturity, beginning at the cap margin and progressing inward. The Inky Cap often forms clusters in grass or woody ground and is found throughout North America during the spring and summer or during the winter in California. The mushroom is edible but may cause illness if eaten with alcohol. Also known as the Alcohol Inky Cap and Tippler's Bane.

Common Psathyrella, *Psathyrella candolleana*
Family: Psathyrellaceae (Ink Caps and others)
Height to 4"
Spore print: Purple-brown

Cap is up to 4" wide, cone-shaped or convex, becoming flattened with age. Surface is smooth, pale yellow-brown or gray-brown, and often has whitish veil remnants along the margin. Stalk is thin, hollow, whitish, and delicate, with a thin collar that is often lost early in development. Gills are attached, white, turning grayish and finally purplish-brown. The Common Psathyrella grows in suburban lawns and gardens throughout North America during the spring and fall. It is edible but insubstantial. Also known as the Suburban Psathyrella.

Pleated Inky Cap, *Parasola plicatilis*
Family: Psathyrellaceae (Ink Caps and others)
Height to 3"
Spore print: Black

This tiny mushroom has a cap up to 1" wide, conical or convex, becoming flattened with age. Flesh is translucent and fragile, colored yellow-brown with a darker, sometimes reddish-brown center, and is well-grooved nearly to the center of the cap. Stalk is white, thin, and delicate. Gills are free but attached to a thin collar just under the cap, pale gray and then black, but not inky like *Coprinus* species. The Pleated Inky Cap is found in grassy areas, gardens, and meadows throughout North America during the spring and summer. It is edible but hardly worth it due to the small size. Also known as the Japanese Umbrella Inky.

Haymaker's Mushroom, *Panaeolus foenisecii*
Family: Bolbitiaceae
Height to 3"
Spore print: Dark brown

This tiny mushroom has a cap up to 1" wide, bell-shaped to convex, becoming somewhat flattened with age. Surface is smooth or can be rough when dry, reddish-brown to tan, and may show a darker band near the margin. Stalk is thin, fragile, long, and whitish to pale brown. Gills are attached, pale brown, becoming dark brown. The Haymaker's Mushroom grows on lawns and grassy fields throughout most of North America during the spring and summer. It is edible but not recommended, and is known to be mildly hallucinogenic.

Brick Top, *Hypholoma lateritium*
Family: Strophariaceae
Height to 4"
Spore print: Dark purple-brown

Cap is up to 3½" wide, convex to flattened, smooth, brick-red or orange in the center, and fading to light brown or yellowish toward the margin. Stalk is pale with some reddish streaking and has a thin, fragile collar that is often missing. Gills are attached, pale yellow, and then grayish and finally purplish-black. Flesh will turn dark upon bruising. The Brick Top grows on rotting wood or humus in eastern North America during the late summer and fall. It is edible and best when young.

Scaly Pholiota, *Pholiota squarrosa* ☠

Family: Strophariaceae
Height to 5"
Spore print: Brown

Cap is up to 4" wide, rounded, and then becoming convex to flattened, and its dry, beige surface is covered with discrete, dark,
upcurved scales. The stalk is thick, with coloring and scaling as
on the cap, and retains veil remnants from a collar near the top.
Gills are attached, pale yellow-green, becoming brown. The Scaly
Pholiota grows on stumps in mixed coniferous or deciduous
woodlands throughout North America during the summer and
fall. Not edible: poisonous!

Common Large Psilocybe, *Psilocybe cubensis*
Family: Hymenogastraceae
Height to 6"
Spore print: Purplish-black

Cap is convex, to 3" wide, white along the margin, yellow to brownish toward the center, and showing some lighter spots. Gills are attached, brown to purple to black. Stalk is white and relatively thin, with some scaling toward the base. The conspicuous collar ring becomes stained purplish-black by falling spores. The Common Large Psilocybe is often seen growing in cattle pastures where dung piles are present, year-round in the Gulf Coast area. Edibility is questionable, and this mushroom is a known hallucinogen.

Dung-loving Psilocybe, *Deconica coprophilia*
Family: Strophariaceae
Height to 2"
Spore print: Purplish-brown

This tiny psilocybe has a convex or flat cap up to 1" wide that is sticky when wet, colored reddish-brown, and has a striated margin. The stalk is thin, equal along its width, pale brown, and may or may not have a collar. Gills are attached, pale brown to purplish-brown. The Dung-loving Psilocybe prefers to grow (you guessed it) in the dung of cattle and is found throughout North America during the summer and fall. It is hallucinogenic. Also known as the Meadow Muffin Mushroom.

Violet Cort, *Cortinarius violaceus*
Family: Cortinariaceae
Height to 7"
Spore print: Reddish-brown

Cap is up to 6" wide, convex, becoming flattened, dry and rough with minute scales, and colored dark purple. The stalk is tough and fibrous, purple, and somewhat enlarged at the base. Like other members of this family, there is a "cortina," or sheath of cobweblike fibers that connects the developing cap margin to the upper stalk. This breaks away in development, sometimes leaving evidence on the stalk or cap margin. Gills are attached and purple. The Violet Cort grows on the ground in coniferous woodlands throughout North America during the fall. It is edible but not great.

Deadly Gallerina, *Gallerina marginata* ☠

Family: Hymenogastraceae

Height to 4"

Spore print: Rusty brown

The cap on this deadly species is up to 2½" wide, convex, becoming flattened, smooth, somewhat sticky when moist, and colored tan to yellow-orange. Stalk is hollow, pale brown above and darker below, and has a thin, membranous collar that may be stained brown by falling spores. Gills are attached, pale yellow-brown, becoming darker with age. The Deadly Gallerina grows on decaying wood in mixed woodlands throughout North America during the spring and fall. It is poisonous and deadly! Also known as the Autumn Gallerina and Deadly Skullcap.

Fawn-colored Pluteus, *Pluteus cervinus*
Family: Pluteaceae
Height to 5"
Spore print: Pink to yellowish-brown
Cap is up to 4" wide, convex or bell-shaped, becoming flattened, gray-brown (deer-colored), lighter at the margin, and has minute, hairy scales around the center. Stalk is pale whitish, even in width, and fibrous. Gills are free, crowded, and white to pinkish. The Fawn-colored Pluteus grows in areas of rotting wood or sawdust, rooting close to the surface, and is found throughout North America during the spring and fall or during the winter in the Southwest. It is edible but best when young and firm. Also known as the Deer Mushroom.

Straw-colored Fiber Head, *Inocybe rimosa* ☠

Family: Inocybaceae

Height to 3"

Spore print: Brown

Cap is up to 3" wide, conical or bell-shaped, becoming flattened with a distinct, raised, central knob. Color is yellowish (straw-colored) with radial fibers that crack open at the margin. Stalk is white or pale brown, fibrous, and equal along its length. Gills are attached or partly attached, whitish, becoming gray-brown. The Straw-colored Fiber Head grows in mixed deciduous or coniferous woodlands throughout North America during the late summer and fall. Not edible: poisonous!

Slimy Gomphidius, *Gomphidius glutinosus*
Family: Gomphidiaceae
Height to 4"
Spore print: Gray to black

Cap is up to 4" wide, convex, becoming flattened and then depressed in the center. Surface is smooth and slimy when wet and colored purplish to grayish-brown, sometimes with darker spots. The stalk is thick, becoming narrower at the base, white above and yellowish below. There is a thin, fibrous, slimy collar, sometimes stained gray with spores, which is often missing in maturity. Gills are thick, descending down the stalk, and pale to dark gray. The Slimy Gomphidius grows on the ground in coniferous woodlands throughout North America during the summer and fall. It is edible but best if the slimy surface is removed first.

Shaggy-stalked Bolete, *Aureoboletus betula*
Family: Boletaceae (Boletes)
Height to 8"
Spore print: Greenish-brown

Cap is up to 3" wide, convex, slimy when wet, and red-orange with a lighter margin. The stalk is long and thin, even along its length, yellow, and covered with shaggy, vertical ridges and grooves. Instead of gills, boletes have a spongy fertile surface under the cap that contains small tubes that open up as pores. In this case, it is colored greenish-yellow and is shrunken around the stalk. The Shaggy-stalked Bolete grows on the ground in mixed woodlands (especially oak) in eastern North America during the late summer and fall. It is edible but not great.

Hollow-stalked Larch Bolete, *Suillus cavipes*
Family: Suillaceae
Height to 3½"
Spore print: Dark greenish-brown

Cap is up to 4" wide, convex, becoming flattened, with a slightly inrolled margin. Surface is colored dark to light rusty orange-brown and covered with tiny, suedelike fibers. Stalk is thick and stubby, hollow at the base, yellow above a membranous collar and rusty below, and paler at the bottom. The spongy tubes and pores of the fertile surface are pale to bright yellow. The Hollow-stalked Larch Bolete is found (you guessed it) near or under larch trees across northern North America during the fall. It is edible and excellent. Also known as the Hollow-stalked Larch Suillus and Hollow Foot.

Zeller's Bolete, *Xerocomellus zelleri*
Family: Boletaceae (Boletes)
Height to 3½"
Spore print: Greenish-brown

Cap is up to 4" wide, convex and then flattened, with a lumpy and wrinkled surface that is dry and powdery, reddish-gray or brownish to nearly black. The stalk is thick and straight, with tan and red streaking like a stalk of rhubarb. The spongy fertile surface of pores and tubes is pale yellow to greenish. Flesh is yellow and may turn blue when bruised. The Zeller's Bolete grows on the ground in coniferous woodlands and near redwoods along the Pacific coast during the summer and fall. It is edible and considered quite good.

King Bolete, *Boletus edulis*
Family: Boletaceae (Boletes)
Height to 10"
Spore print: Greenish-brown

This large bolete has a cap of up to 10" across that is convex to flattened, smooth, and some shade of reddish-brown. The stalk is thick and stout, becoming thicker and bulbous at the base, and colored pale brown with cottony striations on the upper portion. The spongy fertile surface of pores and tubes is white, becoming greenish-yellow or brown. The King Bolete grows on the ground in coniferous and deciduous woodlands throughout North America during the summer and fall. Commonly known as the Porcini, it is edible and highly prized but best if cooked.

Two-colored Bolete, *Baorangia bicolor*
Family: Boletaceae (Boletes)
Height to 5"
Spore print: Greenish-brown

Cap is up to 6" wide, convex, becoming flattened. Surface is dry and rosy-red, turning paler with age. The stalk is thick and short, somewhat thicker near the base, and yellowish above and cap-colored below. The spongy fertile surface of tubes and pores is yellowish. Flesh turns blue upon bruising. The Two-colored Bolete grows in deciduous woodlands, especially oak, in middle and eastern North America during the summer and fall. The mushroom is edible and very good. Also known as the Red and Yellow Bolete.

Slippery Jack, *Suillus luteus*
Family: Suillaceae
Height to 4"
Spore print: Cinnamon-brown

Cap is up to 4½" wide, convex, becoming flattened, various shades of red-orange, brown, or yellow, with a surface that is slimy when wet and shiny even when dry. The stalk is thick, yellowish above and smudged purple below, with a membranous collar that is part whitish and part purplish. The spongy fertile surface under the cap is whitish to yellow, becoming darker with age. There is no color change to the flesh when bruised. The Slippery Jack grows in mixed coniferous woodlands mostly in eastern North America during the fall. It is edible if the slimy surface is first removed.

Old Man of the Woods, *Strobilomyces floccopus*
Family: Boletaceae (Boletes)
Height to 6"
Spore print: Brown or black

Cap is up to 6" wide, convex to flattened, dry, whitish, and covered with dark gray, shaggy scales. The margin may also be shaggy with veil remnants. The stalk is covered in fibrous scales like the cap and has a loose, grayish collar. The spongy fertile surface of tubes and pores is a light gray that turns darker with age. The flesh, when bruised, turns red and then black. The Old Man of the Woods grows in mixed woodlands, especially around oaks, in middle and eastern North America during the summer and fall. It is edible but best when young.

Beefsteak Polypore, *Fistulina hepatica*
Family: Fistulinaceae
Width to 10"
Spore print: Orange-pink

The Beefsteak Polypore is a fleshy, meatlike, semicircular lobe, to 2" thick, pink or reddish-orange to dark red, marked with darker red streaks. The stalk is very short and thick and emerges from one side, forming a kind of shelf for the fungus. Underneath, the tube surface is spongy, pale gray to reddish, and juicy. The Latin name *hepatica* means "liverlike" and describes its appearance. It releases a bloodlike juice when cut. It is found growing on dead or living oaks or other hardwoods, mostly in eastern North America during the summer and fall. The mushroom is edible. Also known as the Ox Tongue Fungus.

Red-belt Fungus, *Formitopsis pinicola*
Family: Fomitopsidaceae
Width to 12"
Spore print: White or yellowish
The Red-belt Fungus is a stemless, convex or hoof-shaped fungus that forms a shelf on dead wood and stumps. It is hard and tough, with concentric rings of brownish-red to black above, bright red near the edge, and white at the margin. The spongy tube and pore surface of the underside is white or pale yellow. The mushroom grows throughout the year in western and northern North America, becoming larger as it adds more material from season to season. Not edible because the flesh is too tough to eat. Also known as the Red-belted Conk and Red-belted Polypore.

Chicken Mushroom, *Laetiporus sulphureus*
Family: Fomitopsidaceae
Width to 20"
Spore print: White

The Chicken Mushroom forms semicircular or clamshell-shaped lobes with a wavy, furrowed margin. Surface is smooth, orange-red, turning pale yellow toward the edge. The spongy underside pore surface is sulfur yellow. There is no stalk; the cap attaches directly to tree trunks or rotting stumps, where it appears singly or in shelflike clusters. The mushroom grows in deciduous or coniferous woodlands throughout North America during the summer and fall. It is edible and very good if cooked, and is said to taste like chicken. Also known as the Sulfur Shelf and Chicken of the Woods.

Turkey Tail, *Trametes versicolor*
Family: Polyporaceae (Polypores and Crust Fungi)
Width to 4"
Spore print: White or pale yellow

The Turkey Tail forms stalkless, semicircular lobes in clusters, making overlapping brackets or shelves on dead wood in mixed woodlands, particularly hardwoods. Flesh is tough and leathery with scalloped margins. Color is quite variable but always arranged in concentric rings or zones of black, brown, gray, and ochre. The fertile underside of tubes and pores is white or pale yellow. The mushroom is found throughout North America during the spring and fall but may persist over the course of several seasons. It is edible but very tough. Also known as the Many-colored Polypore.

Artist's Fungus, *Ganoderma applanatum*
Family: Ganodermataceae
Width to 20"
Spore print: Brown

The Artist's Fungus is stalkless, semicircular or thick like a hoof, and attaches like a shelf to stumps or logs in mixed woodlands. Surface is dry, woody, furrowed, and tough, in various shades of gray or brown in concentric zones, and sometimes covered with orange-brown spore powder. The underside fertile surface consists of tightly packed spongy pores, whitish, turning dark when bruised. Hence, it can be etched on to create messages or drawings. The mushroom appears in all seasons throughout North America. It is not edible due to its tough and woody texture. Also known as the Artist's Conk.

Shingled Hedgehog, *Sarcodon imbricatus*
Family: Bankeraceae
Height to 4"
Spore print: Brown

Cap is up to 8" wide, convex to flattened and then depressed in the center. Surface is dull brown and covered with rough, dark brown scales, which are sometimes pointed and raised. The stalk is whitish or pale brown and quite short. The underside, spore-producing surface is composed of pale gray spines or needles that descend down the stalk and turn darker with age. The Shingled Hedgehog grows on the ground in deciduous or coniferous woodlands throughout North America during the late spring and fall. It is edible but not great. Also known as the Scaly Tooth and Scaly Hydnum.

Bear's Head Tooth, *Hericium coralloides*
Family: Hericiaceae
Width to 18"
Spore print: White

The Bear's Head Tooth forms a network of fleshy, white, or creamy brown branching structures that terminate with drooping, icicle-like spines to ½" long. Clumps of these formations attach to dead logs or stumps in hardwood forests by means of an indistinct, clinging base. The mushroom is found in northeastern North America during the summer and fall, although similar species are found in the West. It is edible and very good but quite rare. Also known as the Waterfall Hydnum or Coral Tooth Fungus.

Cauliflower Mushroom, *Sparassis radicata*
Family: Sparassidaceae
Width to 24"
Spore print: White

The Cauliflower Mushroom forms a large mound that is cauliflower-shaped but more ribbonlike or noodlelike in density, covered with fleshy, tough, wavy lobes. It is white to pale yellow-brown and supported by a stout stalk that penetrates deeply into the substrate. The mushroom is mostly found at the base of trees in coniferous forests throughout North America during the fall. It is edible and excellent when cooked to make it tender.

Spindle Coral, *Clavulinopsis fusiformis*
Family: Clavariaceae (Coral Fungi)
Height to 6"
Spore print: White
The Spindle Coral forms thin, erect, fragile, spindle-shaped clubs, somewhat like vertical worms, that are yellow-orange and fuse to a common base. They are often forked or flattened along their length. Spores are produced over the entire spindle surface. The mushroom grows in grassy areas and mixed woodlands in eastern North America and California during the late summer and fall. It is edible but insubstantial.

Shaggy Chanterelle, *Turbinellus floccosus*
Family: Gomphaceae
Height to 8"
Spore print: Ochre

The Shaggy Chanterelle begins as a blunt cylinder and becomes vase- or funnel-shaped with a wavy margin. The inner surface is yellow-orange to red-orange and filled with wooly, fibrous scales that peel upward. The fertile, outside surface is composed of cream to pale yellow-orange longitudinal veins that reach from cap to base. The mushroom is found in coniferous woodlands and mountainous areas throughout North America during the summer and fall. It is edible but not recommended. Also known as the Scaly Vase Chanterelle and Wooly Chanterelle.

Golden Chanterelle, *Cantharellus cibarius*
Family: Cantharellaceae
Height to 4"
Spore print: Pale yellow-brown

Cap is up to 6" wide, convex, and then flattened with a sunken center and a wavy, lobed margin. Surface is smooth and pale tan to orange-yellow. The fertile underside is a network of pale yellowish ridges extending from the cap to midway down the stalk. The flesh has a subtle, fruity odor and spicy taste. The Golden Chanterelle is found in oak or coniferous woodlands throughout North America during the summer in the East, fall in the Northwest, and winter in California. It is edible and choice, but be careful not to confuse it with the toxic Jack-o-lantern mushroom.

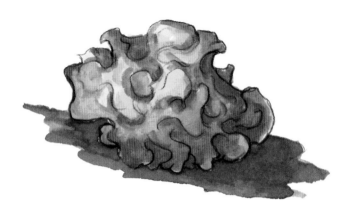

Witch's Butter, *Tremella mesenterica*
Family: Tremellaceae
Width to 8"
Spore print: Pale yellow

Witch's Butter is a yellow-orange, gelatinous mass, brainlike in shape with fleshy, curling lobes. It becomes very tough and hard when dry but may swell and become an amorphous blob during wet periods. The mushroom grows year-round in mixed deciduous woodlands, mostly on dead wood, throughout North America. It is edible but insubstantial, being mostly water. Also known as the Golden Jelly Fungus.

Ochre Jelly Club, *Leotia lubrica*
Family: Leotiaceae
Height to 2"

Head is up to ¾" wide, convex, and variously lobed and crinkled. Surface is smooth, yellow-ochre to reddish- or greenish-brown. Stalk is colored as the cap, smooth or with tiny scales. Spores are produced on the cap. It grows on the ground in areas of rotting wood in mixed woodlands and sometimes forms huge clusters. The Ochre Jelly Club is found throughout North America during the summer and fall. Not edible, due to its unappealing texture. Also known as the Jelly Baby.

Earthstar, *Geastrum triplex* ☠

Family: Geastraceae (Earthstars)

Width to 4"

Spore print: Brown

The Earthstar is a pale brownish, bulbous fruiting mass whose outer wall splits apart, forming four to eight raylike arms, sometimes cracking, that resemble a kind of flower. The central, spore-containing sac is grayish to pale brownish-red, pointed at the top, and rests on a saucerlike base. The mushroom grows near leaf litter or humus under trees in mixed deciduous woodlands throughout North America during the late summer or fall. Not edible. Also known as the Collared Earthstar.

Giant Puffball, *Calvatia gigantea*
Family: Agaricaceae
Width to 20" or more
Spore print: White, turning olive-brown

The Giant Puffball is a huge, white, spherical or irregularly lobed mass with skin that is smooth and leathery when young but eventually becomes brittle and peels away to reveal the inner section and spore mass. There is no stalk, only a rootlike myce-lium on the underside. Some western forms may show scaling on the surface. The mushroom grows during the spring through fall in eastern North America in a variety of habitats, including open woodlands and grassy areas, and may form fairy rings. It is edible and very good, especially when young.

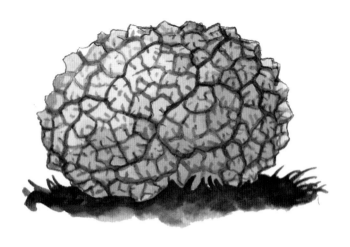

Sculptured Puffball, *Calbovista subsculpta*
Family: Agaricaceae
Width to 6"
Spore print: White, turning greenish-brown

The Sculptured Puffball is shaped like a ball or an inverted pear, whitish or pale brown, with a surface broken into irregular, angular raised scales with a center containing small hairs. The base is stubby and connects to the ground via mycelial filaments. The mushroom is found at high elevations of the Pacific mountains and the Rocky Mountains in coniferous woodlands or grassy areas during the spring, summer, and fall. Edible when it is young and the spores are white. Also known as the Warted Giant Puffball.

Poison Puffball, *Scleroderma aurantium* ☠
Family: Sclerodermataceae
Width to 4"
Spore print: Violet-gray to black

The Poison Puffball is spherical but wider than tall, yellowish-brown, with an outer skin or "peridium" that is tough, leathery, and cracked into segments with a dark, central wart. Eventually it cracks away to reveal the dark spore mass inside. It adheres to the substrate with a short, thick base. The mushroom is found in a variety of woodlands or grassy areas and gardens throughout North America during the late summer and fall. Not edible: poisonous! Also known as the Common Earthball and Thick-skinned Puffball.

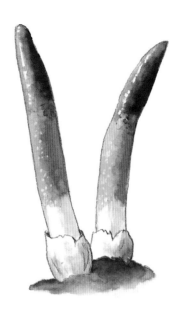

Elegant Stinkhorn, *Mutinus elegans*
Family: Phallaceae (Stinkhorns)
Height to 7"

The Elegant Stinkhorn begins as a small, whitish egg, from which the fruiting body emerges to form a tall, slender stalk that tapers at the apex. The surface is minutely bumpy, rosy-pink above and white or pale yellow-orange below. The spore mass is a greenish-brown coating that covers the upper part of the stalk, eventually becoming a liquid slime. At the base of the stalk is a saclike volva, which is the remnant of the initial egg stage. The mushroom grows near rotting wood in gardens, fields, and woodlands in eastern North America during the late summer and fall. It is edible in the egg stage.

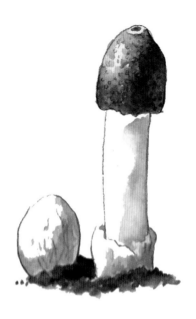

Ravenel's Stinkhorn, *Phallus ravenelii* ☠

Family: Phallaceae (Stinkhorns)

Height to 7"

Fruiting body begins as an egg-shaped mass from which emerges the stalk and head. Head is bulbous or conical, somewhat grainy, and covered in a slimy, green coating. At the apex is a small, whitish spot that opens to the tip of the stalk. Stalk is even along its length, white to pale yellow, with a white or pinkish, membranous basal cup or volva. The spores are embedded in the slime that covers the head, and insects attracted to its foul odor disperse the spores. The Ravenel's Stinkhorn grows in rotting wood, humus, and sawdust piles in eastern North America during the fall. Not edible.

Black Morel, *Morchella elata*
Family: Morchellaceae (Morels and allies)
Height to 4"

Fruiting body is up to 2" wide, elongated, bullet-shaped, or oval, colored various shades of dark brown or gray. Surface is a network of smooth ribs, mostly longitudinal down the cap, that borders yellowish-brown pits. Stalk is stout, smooth, whitish, and bulbous at the base. Both the cap and stalk are hollow. Spores are yellow-brown and located in the pits between the ribs. The Black Morel grows in mixed coniferous and deciduous woodlands, especially areas of recent fire, throughout North America during the spring. Edible and choice but must be cooked.

Common Morel, *Morchella esculenta*
Family: Morchellaceae (Morels and allies)
Height to 6"

Upper portion is a variable, elongated egg or bullet shape to 2" wide. Surface is like a sponge, honeycombed with irregular, pale to deep ochre ridges and dark brown pits. The stubby stalk is white, somewhat crinkly or bumpy, with a thick base. Spores in this group are produced not in gills but rather in structures known as asci, located in the pits. They are responsible for the deeper yellow color of the morel at maturity. The Common Morel grows from spring to summer in a variety of wooded habitats, including orchards and gardens, and is found throughout North America. It is highly edible and prized. Also known as the Yellow Morel and Honeycomb Morel.

Half-free Morel, *Morchella semilibera*
Family: Morchellaceae (Morels and allies)
Height to 5"

This is a true morel with a roundish to conical cap to 2" wide, with the lower one-third to two-thirds of the cap free from the stalk. Cap is light to dark brown with deep pits and ridges. Initially, the ridges are about the same pale brown as the pits but become nearly black with age. Stalk is roughly equal in diameter along its length (or with a bulbous base), whitish, rough-textured with small granules, and hollow in cross section. The Half-free Morel is found alone or in groups, often under hardwood trees near streams, fruiting early in the spring before other morels. It is edible and quite good.

Bell Morel, *Verpa conica*
Family: Morchellaceae (Morels and allies)
Height to 5"

This is not a true morel of the genus *Morchella*, but a related mushroom of the genus *Verpa*. The small cap is smooth, lobed, or slightly wrinkled—not with raised ridges. It is shaped like a dome, bell, or thimble, colored light to dark brown, and attached to the stalk only at the apex, hanging freely. The stalk is whitish to tan and mostly smooth or with a faint grainy texture, and is partially hollow with a cottony pith. The Bell Morel is found during the spring in riparian woodlands or near conifers. It is edible but not substantial. Also known as the Thimble Morel.

False Morel, *Verpa bohemica*
Family: Morchellaceae (Morels and allies)
Height to 6"

The False Morel is similar in appearance to the Half-free Morel, but the cap is attached only at the very top of the stalk and hangs loosely on it. The cap is proportionately small, rounded like an upside-down thimble, colored tan to dark brown (or black with old specimens). It is wrinkled with vertically oriented ridges, less obviously "pitted" than a true morel. The stalk is creamy white to tan, uniform along its length, and filled with a cottony pith (sometimes lacking with age). The False Morel is found in wooded areas, especially near streams, during early spring—sometimes it is called the Early Morel. It is edible, but not generally prized, and may cause stomach upset for some.

Devil's Cup, *Urnula craterium*
Family: Sarcosomataceae (Cup Fungi)
Height to 5"

The Devil's Cup is, as the name suggests, urn- or cup-shaped, thin, leathery, with a slightly inrolled margin. The inner, spore-producing surface is fairly smooth and dark brown or black. The outer surface is rough, grayish pink to dark gray, and sometimes hairy. The stalk is small and thin, tapering to a ragged, rooting mass. The cup begins closed and opens upon maturity. The Devil's Cup often grows in clusters in deciduous woodlands and near oaks in eastern North America during the spring. Not edible, due to its unappealing texture. Also known as the Crater's Cup or Devil's Urn.

Stalked Scarlet Cup, *Sarcoscypha occidentalis*
Family: Sarcoscyphaceae
Height to 1"
The tiny Stalked Scarlet Cup forms a smooth, thin, shallow, nearly translucent red-orange or scarlet-colored cup. The undersurface is white and smooth and merges with the stalk. It prefers to grow on dead wood and fallen branches in moist, deciduous woodlands. The mushroom is found in eastern North America during the spring and summer. Not edible; far too insubstantial.

Snowbank Orange Peel Fungus, *Caloscypha fulgens*
Family: Pyronemataceae
Height to 1"

This very colorful, tiny fungus has a minimal or absent stalk. The cap is shaped like a little cup, quite rounded, becoming flatter and wavy with age. The color is a brilliant orange overall, with darker bluish-green areas appearing along the cup margins. It forms little groups in moist or boggy spots under conifers, often near melting snow-fields, where it is parasitic on pine and spruce seeds. The Snowbank Orange Peel Fungus is found across North America, particularly in western mountains, beginning in early spring following the snow-melt. Not substantial enough to be edible.

Bird's Nest Fungus, *Cyathus striatus*
Family: Nidulariaceae
Height to ¾"

Bird's Nest Fungus forms tiny cups to ½" wide, like little nests in the shape of an inverted cone, wide on top and narrow at the base. Inner surface is shiny, reddish-brown, with broad grooves. Outer surface is dark brown and covered with shaggy hairs. Inside the cup reside several whitish "eggs" or spore-containing sacs that are ejected by the force of raindrops entering the cup. In early stages a whitish membrane covers the cup. The fungus often forms dense groups in open woodlands, rotting wood, and sawdust piles throughout North America during the late summer and fall. Not substantial enough to be edible.

Index

About the Author/Illustrator

Todd Telander is a natural-ist illustrator/artist living in Walla Walla, Washington. He has studied and illustrated wildlife for the last thirty-five years while living in California, Colorado, New Mexico, and Washington. He graduated from the University of California at Santa Cruz with degrees in biology, environmental studies, and scientific illustration and has since illustrated numerous books and other publications, including FalconGuides' Scats and Tracks series. In addition, he is an established landscape painter and art teacher. He and his wife, Kirsten Telander, a writer, own a small art gallery in Walla Walla called the Telander Gallery. He has two sons, Miles and Oliver, both pursuing creative careers. His work can be viewed online at www.toddtelander.com.